The Blessings of Being
Under Spiritual Authority

The Blessings of Being Under Spiritual Authority

■ ■ ■

Emmanuel Adewusi

Scriptures taken from New King James Version. Copyright 1979, 1980, 1982 by Thomas Nelson, Inc. Used by permission. All right reserved.

Author: Emmanuel Adewusi
Cover Design: Timothy Paul Designs
ISBN-13: 9780995349223
ISBN-10: 0995349223

Table of Contents

Preface

There are many books out there that talk about Spiritual Authority. They all approach spiritual authority from the perspective of a believer exercising their God-given authority and power over situations, spiritual forces, attacks from the enemy and so on and so forth. This book takes a different approach, by addressing the lack of spiritual authority. Perhaps, some believers are aware of their God-given authority. Perhaps, they even try to exercise that authority to no avail. This could be because many Christians do not appreciate the need for being under authority, hence are not under anyone's authority, hence their inability to exercise their God-given authority.

This book goes beyond espousing the need for mentorship and the benefits of it. It explains what it means to be under spiritual authority. It breaks down what real spiritual authority looks like and how to spot counterfeit authority. It explains the excesses that may arise from misunderstanding and misapplying the wisdom from this book. It shows how to remain under the right spiritual authority, among other insights.

You might have been previously scarred by being under a wrong kind of spiritual authority. This does not mean the best thing to do is not to have one anymore. There are many fake currencies out there, but it does not stop us from accepting money for fear of it being fake. Release your heart to God again, trust Him and He will lead you to the right spiritual authority.

Caution: Before you begin to apply the contents of this book, ensure you read the entire book. It is critical that your understanding is balanced and well-rounded before you begin to apply the wisdom from this book. Not heeding this recommendation can have undesired consequences.

Dedication

To my personal Lord and Savior, Jesus Christ. You demonstrated excellence in nurturing the apostles to live a victorious Christian life.

To my ever-present helper, The Holy Spirit. You are the one working through me, enabling me to be and do all that God desires for me.

To my wife, Ibukun, for your constant love and tireless support.

To my mentor, Rev. Dike Odimuko, for allowing yourself to be the vessel God used to expose me to Spiritual Authority. In 2012, while visiting in Ottawa, I was excited to tell you that I would be enrolling at Oral Roberts Bible Institute. Since I was not sure of what to expect during the Bible school, I decided to ask you to recommend courses that will be of benefit to me. As is characteristic of you, you said "Brother Emmanuel, I think you should take a course on Spiritual Authority. It will help you a lot". That stuck, and even though I could not enroll in a course like that at school, I immediately began learning more about Spiritual Authority. Thank you for pointing me in this direction Sir!

To every leader, volunteer and member of Cornerstone Christian Church of God, for demonstrating to me that Spiritual Authority works. I can see the blessings of spiritual authority in your lives.

I

Spiritual Authority

Earlier in my life, I found it difficult to submit to spiritual authority because I did not understand why I needed to submit to someone. I neither understood that being under spiritual authority was for my benefit, nor did I grasp the fact that God has reserved blessings for those who choose to be under spiritual authority. The truth is, God requires us to be under spiritual authority and God's commands are not grievous. As you read this book, I pray it will open your eyes to "what's in it for you".

I had an encounter with God that enhanced my understanding of being under spiritual authority. I was asking God for the grace to be humble, and after I finished praying, the Holy Spirit spoke to me. He simply said, "You are struggling with submission to authority because you are focusing on what you think you will lose (i.e. your right to do anything you want to do). Begin to focus on the blessings of being under spiritual authority and it will become easier for you to go all the way, in being under spiritual authority". This truth that was revealed by the Holy Spirit truly set me free. I am thriving, happy, free, and blessed being under spiritual authority.

The truth is that where the Spirit of God is, there is liberty. You become truly free when you are under God's direct and indirect spiritual authority. From today, I pray that you are set free from every bondage and wrong thinking that is hindering your submission to God. May God lead you to the right human spiritual authority to submit to and give you the grace to abide there.

What is Spiritual Authority?

The Merriam - Webster Dictionary has many definitions for authority. The most relevant definitions are:

- "power to influence or command thought, opinion, or behavior
- persons in command; specifically, i.e. government

- a governmental agency or corporation to administer a revenue-producing public enterprise for example, the transit authority"

Authority never means someone having a passive influence over you, it implies active influence. This is why it is a sensitive topic that one must approach with caution and godly reverence. Even though it has been repeatedly abused by some, that does not make it wrong. An authority is someone you have given control over you and the affairs of your life. That person has the right to influence and direct you.

There are many authorities in the world today. There are government agencies, law enforcement agencies, boards, commissions and United Nations. All these are examples of organizations setup by a governing body, to control the actions of people one way or the other. We have become used to them being around, that we do not consciously realize the influence they have.

One kind of authority that is constantly being attacked and kicked against is spiritual authority. Spiritual authority is the foundation for all other authority to properly function. When spiritual authority is properly instituted, other authorities do not have a hard time functioning.

Emmanuel Adewusi

Spiritual authority is being under God's authority directly or indirectly (human). It is the kind of authority you submit your will to, because such an authority is under the authority of God.

Your spiritual authority is one you have submitted to and you have accepted to be greater than you, because such authority is under God's authority.

An example of submitting one's will to another greater than them is found in the account of Mary in Luke 1:38

> *Then Mary said, "Behold the maidservant of the Lord! Let it be to me according to your word." And the angel departed from her.*

This statement made by Mary clearly shows that she put the direction of her life and future under the proclamation that the angel delivered to her from God. She did not challenge or argue with the Word. Indeed, these are the words of a person under spiritual authority. Let it be to me according to your word! Praise God! Unlike other kinds of authority, spiritual authority is not meant to be taken from a person, but to be given by a person to another. When we truly accept Jesus into our heart, what we are simply saying is that we are giving Jesus Christ the spiritual authority to control our lives. Instead of you just doing what you feel like doing, you now strive to do only what pleases the Lord Jesus Christ.

Satan Violated God's Authority

"How you are fallen from heaven, O Lucifer, son of the morning! How you are cut down to the ground, you who weakened the nations! For you have said in your heart: 'I will ascend into heaven, I will exalt my throne above the stars of God; I will also sit on the mount of the congregation on the farthest sides of the north; I will ascend above the heights of the clouds, I will be like the Most High.' Yet you shall be brought down to Sheol, to the lowest depths of the Pit" (Isaiah 14:12-15).

From the above scripture, we see that satan was not content with serving God. He wanted to be God. As a result of that pride in his heart, he became rebellious. Perhaps, his beauty led him to believe that humans and angels ought to worship him instead of God. Perhaps, he felt that he had served God enough and it was time for him to "enjoy".

Pride always leads to a fall and you can never be under spiritual authority without the virtue of humility. Humility enables you to gracefully submit your will to another.

Spiritual Authority Explained Further

Many people think they are under authority, just because they have identified someone that ought to be their spiritual authority. The Centurion in the Bible, taught us what spiritual authority ought to look like. According to him, those under his authority can be told to go and they will go, come and they will come, be still and such will be done. There can be no spiritual authority without submission. It is impossible to be under spiritual authority without ultimate, total and complete control by the one who is your spiritual authority.

> *The centurion answered and said, "Lord, I am not worthy that You should come under my roof. But only speak a word, and my servant will be healed. For I also am a man under authority, having soldiers under me. And I say to this one, 'Go,' and he goes; and to another, 'Come,' and he comes; and to my servant, 'Do this,' and he does it" (Matthew 8:8-9).*

The military is one institution that consistently records success in almost every country in the world. One possible reason is that they absolutely understand the principle of being under authority. In military terminology, being under authority is referred to as the "chain of command". According to Online Business Dictionary, chain of command is defined as:

"The order in which authority and power in an organization is wielded and delegated from top management to every employee at every level of the organization. Instructions flow downward along the chain of command and accountability flows upward."

"According to its proponent Henri Fayol (1841-1925), the more clear cut the chain of command, the more effective the decision making process and greater the efficiency. Military forces are an example of straight chain of command that extends in unbroken line from the top brass to ranks. Also called, line of command."

The concept of hierarchy is clearly understood. Soldiers understand that they do not all have the same level of command. Soldiers are expected to obey orders from superiors, even when they do not agree. Everyone signs up with the military clearly understands that what your superior asks you to do must be done without questions or hesitation. The Bible often likens a Christian to a soldier or a warrior that wears an armor.

> *No soldier in active service entangles himself in the affairs of everyday life, so that he may please the one who enlisted him as a soldier (II Timothy 2:4).*
>
> *Therefore, take up the full armor of God, so that you will be able to resist in the evil day, and having done everything, to stand firm (Ephesians 6:13).*

Until the body of Christ clearly begins to function like the military (with the Holy Spirit as the head of the army) and resist attempts by the devil to cause a mutiny or rebellion, it will never be able to function effectively and efficiently at its peak.

Spiritual authority is God's way of governing the earth that He created. God's plan is that in every gathering of His children, there is a clear human spiritual authority through which His plans and purposes are known and followed. The human race and the animal kingdom are to be governed by clearly established lines of authority.

Asides from God directly instructing us to be under spiritual authority from scriptures, there are many other ways He indirectly validates the concept of human spiritual authority. Here are a few.

The way He addresses people:

- He validated that Hezekiah was under authority by saying He was the God of David his father.
  - ○ *"Return and tell Hezekiah the leader of My people, 'Thus says the LORD, the God of David your father: "I have heard your prayer, I have seen your tears; surely I will heal you. On the third day you shall go up to the house of the LORD" (II Kings 20:5).*

The way He introduces Himself to people:

- He validated spiritual authority to Moses by the way He introduced Himself to him
  - ○ *"Then He said, "Do not draw near this place. Take your sandals off your feet, for the place where you stand is holy ground." Moreover He said, "I am the God of your father—the God of Abraham, the God of Isaac, and the God of Jacob." And Moses hid his face, for he was afraid to look upon God" (Exodus 3:5-6).*

The fact that He answers their prayers when they invoke the name of their spiritual authority.

- He validated spiritual authority by answering Elisha when he called on the God of his spiritual father, Elijah. In this instance, Elisha just received a double portion of his departed spiritual father, Elijah. The first miracle he performed was by calling on God to answer him, just like He answered Elijah in parting the river. The fact that the river parted as he desired, meant that God honored the memory of Elijah and also acknowledged that Elisha was a bonafide spiritual son of Elijah.
   - *"Then he took the mantle of Elijah that had fallen from him, and struck the water, and said, "Where is the LORD God of Elijah?" And when he also had struck the water, it was divided this way and that; and Elisha crossed over" (II Kings 2:14).*

What Submission to Authority is NOT

Lord Acton once said: 'Power tends to corrupt and absolute power corrupts absolutely. When power is left unchecked, it has the potential to corrupt — even someone that has good intentions.

Many people have accepted a path of rebellion, because they have witnessed or heard of human spiritual authorities abusing their authority. I understand where they are coming from, but it is an unsubstantial reason to miss out on the blessings of being under spiritual authority.

Submission to spiritual authority does not mean:

- An inability to reason for yourself.
  - o God even said *"Come let us reason together" in Isaiah 1:18.* Anybody who does not allow you to reason for yourself when it is needed is keeping you in bondage. That is not godly, and you must get out of from under that spiritual authority.
- An inability to disobey your spiritual authority if need be.
  - o It is interesting that in II Kings 2:1-8, Elisha disobeyed his spiritual father's instruction to remain in a particular place three times. Elisha was not punished for that disobedience, possibly because he was acting in love, not out of a rebellious intention.

- An inability to think and act based on what God has said to you.
  - In I Kings 13, a prophet died because he put another prophet's instruction above that of God. When you are sure that God has said something to you, that is the instruction that must be followed, not what another man or woman says.
- Allowing an abusive relationship to thrive because he or she is your human spiritual authority.
  - There is a difference between being under a loving spiritual authority and being in an abusive relationship. A spiritual authority from God will love you and help you grow, and not consistently tear you down — to reduce your self-esteem, self-worth or self-confidence.
- Submitting to everyone that has a spiritual title such as: pastor, prophet, apostle, evangelist and such offices.
  - We are instructed in scriptures to test all spirits I John 4:1-3. This is because not everyone that has a spiritual title is operating in the Holy Spirit.
- Being forced into bondage by your spiritual authority
  - Being under spiritual authority is a choice you will make for yourself. No one should "snatch"

your will from you. Anyone that forces or manipulates you to yield your will to them, is not operating in the Spirit of God. Even Jesus said that God did not take His life from Him but He Jesus, gave it up Himself (John 10:18). Anyone who uses scriptures to "beat or harass you into submission" is not operating in the Holy Spirit. You have not been given a bondage again to fear (Romans 8:15). If you are paralyzed by fear when you are with your human spiritual authority or if you are paralyzed in fear when supposedly under the authority of the "spirit" or a "word", check it, as that might not be from God. We also understand from I Peter 5:3 that we are not to lord our authority over others.

- A person taking the place of God in your life
  - God is a jealous God and He will never share His glory with any man (Isaiah 42:8). You can honor man but no one must take the place of God in your life. The Bible even says, "cursed is the man who trusts in man…" Jeremiah 17:5. Understand that being under human (God-ordained) spiritual authority does not mean that you do not need God anymore.

As you continue to read on, you will realize where you might have missed it, with regards to being under spiritual authority. Even though it is a blessing and ordained by God, it can easily become a curse, if not done in accordance with godly principles.

II

Jesus Christ and The Holy Spirit Did It

Jesus Christ Submitted to God the Father and the Holy Spirit

Jesus Christ knew the benefits of being under spiritual authority and He demonstrated that during His earthly ministry.

If you are a Christian, you are one, because you have accepted that Jesus Christ is God. Let us remind ourselves why we believe Jesus is God.

It was Prophesied

There were many witnesses that foretold the birth of God in human form, long before Jesus was born.

Isaiah Prophesied:

"Therefore the Lord himself shall give you a sign; Behold, a virgin shall conceive, and bear a son, and shall call his name Immanuel" (Isaiah 7:14).

For unto us a child is born, unto us a son is given: and the government shall be upon his shoulder: and his name shall be called Wonderful, Counsellor, The mighty God, The everlasting Father, The Prince of Peace. Of the increase of his government and peace there shall be no end, upon the throne of David, and upon his kingdom, to order it, and to establish it with judgment and with justice from henceforth even forever. The zeal of the Lord of hosts will perform this (Isaiah 9:6-7).

Micah Prophesied:

"But you, Bethlehem Ephrathah, Though you are little among the thousands of Judah, Yet out of you shall come forth to Me The One to be Ruler in Israel, Whose goings forth are from of old, From everlasting" (Micah 5:2).

Many witnesses confirmed Jesus Christ as God after His birth

God spoke directly when Jesus was being baptized.

And the Holy Spirit descended in bodily form like a dove upon Him, and a voice came from heaven which said, "You are My beloved Son; in You I am well pleased" (Luke 3:22).

Angels were sent to shepherds to announce the arrival of Jesus Christ

"Now there were in the same country shepherds living out in the fields, keeping watch over their flock by night. And behold, an angel of the Lord stood before them, and the glory of the Lord shone around them, and they were greatly afraid. Then the angel said to them, "Do not be afraid, for behold, I bring you good tidings of great joy which will be to all people. For there is born to you this day in the city of David a Savior, who is Christ the Lord. And this will be the sign to you: You will find a Babe wrapped in swaddling cloths, lying in a manger." And suddenly there was with the angel a multitude of the heavenly host praising God and saying: "Glory to God in the highest, And on earth peace, goodwill toward men!" (Luke 2:8-14)

Simeon confirmed Jesus as the Christ:

"And behold, there was a man in Jerusalem whose name was Simeon, and this man was just and devout, waiting for the Consolation of Israel, and the Holy Spirit was upon him. And it had been revealed to him by the Holy Spirit that he would not see death before he had seen the Lord's Christ. So he came by the Spirit into the temple. And when the parents brought in the Child Jesus, to do for Him according to the custom of the law, he took Him up in his arms and blessed God and said: "Lord, now You are letting Your servant depart in peace, According to Your word; For my eyes have seen Your salvation Which You have prepared before the face of all peoples, A light to bring revelation to the Gentiles, And the glory of Your people Israel" (Luke 2:25-32).

John the Baptist confirmed Jesus as the Christ

"The next day John saw Jesus coming toward him, and said, "Behold! The Lamb of God who takes away the sin of the world! This is He of whom I said, 'After me comes a Man who is preferred before me, for He was before me.' I did not know Him; but that He should be revealed to Israel, therefore I came baptizing with water."And John bore witness,

saying, "I saw the Spirit descending from heaven like a dove, and He remained upon Him. I did not know Him, but He who sent me to baptize with water said to me, 'Upon whom you see the Spirit descending, and remaining on Him, this is He who baptizes with the Holy Spirit.' And I have seen and testified that this is the Son of God" (John 1:29-34).

Peter confirmed Jesus as the Christ

"Simon Peter answered and said, "You are the Christ, the Son of the living God" (Matthew 16:16)

We also understand from John 1:1-4 that Jesus Christ is God in the flesh.

In the beginning was the Word, and the Word was with God, and the Word was God. He was in the beginning with God. All things were made through Him, and without Him nothing was made that was made. In Him was life, and the life was the light of men. (John 1:1-4).

Since we have established from scriptures that Jesus is God, let's now begin to see how even though He is God, He submitted to the authority of God the Father and the Holy Spirit. As God, Jesus Christ had the authority to do anything He wanted to do. He however chose to do only what His spiritual authority did and instructed him to do.

> *Then Jesus answered and said to them, "Most assuredly, I say to you, the Son can do nothing of Himself, but what He sees the Father do; for whatever He does, the Son also does in like manner* (John 5:19).

> *I can of Myself do nothing. As I hear, I judge; and My judgment is righteous, because I do not seek My own will but the will of the Father who sent Me* (John 5:30).

As God, Jesus Christ had the authority to say anything He wanted to say and it will be established. He however chose to say only what His spiritual authority wanted Him to say.

> *Jesus answered them and said, "My doctrine is not Mine, but His who sent Me. If anyone wills to do His will, he shall know concerning the doctrine, whether it is from God or whether I speak on My own authority. He who speaks from himself seeks his own glory; but He who seeks the glory of the One who sent Him*

is true, and no unrighteousness is in Him. Did not Moses give you the law, yet none of you keeps the law? Why do you seek to kill Me?" (John 7:16-19)

Jesus demonstrated he was under spiritual authority even to the point of death, by saying: Father, if thou be willing, remove this cup from me: nevertheless not my will, but thine, be done (Luke 22:42).

Jesus knew that only a person truly under spiritual authority can demonstrate their authority as a believer. For Him to walk in authority on the earth, He needed to be under spiritual authority. That was why He could come back to say all authority has now been given to Him. Praise God, He met the conditions for Him to be in authority.

And Jesus came and spoke to them, saying, "All authority has been given to Me in heaven and on earth (Matthew 18:18).

Jesus earned the authority that He received after demonstrating He could be humble enough to be under spiritual authority.

Let this mind be in you which was also in Christ Jesus, who, being in the form of God, did not consider it robbery to be equal with God, but made Himself of no reputation, taking the form of a bondservant, and coming in the likeness of men. And being found in appearance as a man, He humbled Himself and became obedient to the point of death, even the death of the cross. Therefore God also has highly exalted Him and given Him the name which is above every name, that at the name of Jesus every knee should bow, of those in heaven, and of those on earth, and of those under the earth, and that every tongue should confess that Jesus Christ is Lord, to the glory of God the Father (Philippians 2:5-11).

I encourage and charge you to remain under godly spiritual authority and watch God enthrone you with spiritual authority.

The Holy Spirit submitted to God the Father and Jesus Christ

During Jesus' earthly ministry, He was under the spiritual authority of the Holy Spirit and God the Father.

However, Jesus made it clear that once He ascended to heaven and the Holy Spirit came to dwell in man, the

Holy Spirit will now be under His authority and God the Father's authority.

> *"But now I go away to Him who sent Me, and none of you asks Me, 'Where are You going?' But because I have said these things to you, sorrow has filled your heart. Nevertheless I tell you the truth. It is to your advantage that I go away; for if I do not go away, the Helper will not come to you; but if I depart, I will send Him to you. And when He has come, He will convict the world of sin, and of righteousness, and of judgment: of sin, because they do not believe in Me; of righteousness, because I go to My Father and you see Me no more; of judgment, because the ruler of this world is judged. "I still have many things to say to you, but you cannot bear them now. However, when He, the Spirit of truth, has come, He will guide you into all truth; for He will not speak on His own authority, but whatever He hears He will speak; and He will tell you things to come. He will glorify Me, for He will take of what is Mine and declare it to you. All things that the Father has are Mine. Therefore I said that He will take of Mine and declare it to you (John 16:5-15).*

Emmanuel Adewusi

If the Holy Spirit could submit to Jesus Christ's spiritual authority, it means that you and I ought to be under spiritual authority as well.

III

Spiritual Authority Through the Eyes of the Giants of Faith

We mentioned earlier that spiritual authority is being under God's authority directly or indirectly. It is the kind of authority you submit your will to, because such authority is under the authority of God.

Your spiritual authority is one you have submitted your will to and you have accepted to be greater than you because such authority is under God's authority.

Faith Giant 1 - Abraham

Abraham is referred to as the father of faith and this is because of the life of obedience that he lived. Living under spiritual authority is a great act of faith. Allowing God's direct or indirect authority to direct the course of your life is a great act of faith. Let's walk in Abraham's footsteps to understand why he is known as the father of faith.

Abraham is introduced to us in scriptures in Genesis 11:27-32. In chapter 12 verse 3, we see God instructing him to get out of his country and family and tying a blessing to that act of obedience. In chapter 12 verse 4, the Bible says Abraham departed as the Lord had spoken to him. In this instance, Abraham demonstrated his submission to God's authority.

God tells Abraham to do something that will be very painful, but because Abraham was under spiritual authority, he obeyed immediately. God asked him to circumcise himself and other males in his home, and he obeyed God that same day. I personally know how painful circumcision is to a child, how much more a grown up man. In Genesis 34, there is a story about a group of people that were circumcised and remained in pain for three days. With this understanding, you can imagine the pain Abraham and his household had to endure in order to obey God's circumcision instruction.

And God said to Abraham: "As for you, you shall keep My covenant, you and your descendants after you throughout their generations. This is My covenant which you shall keep, between Me and you and your descendants after you: Every male child among you shall be circumcised; and you shall be circumcised in the flesh of your foreskins, and it shall be a sign of the covenant between Me and you. He who is eight days old among you shall be circumcised, every male child in your generations, he who is born in your house or bought with money from any foreigner who is not your descendant. He who is born in your house and he who is bought with your money must be circumcised, and My covenant shall be in your flesh for an everlasting covenant. And the uncircumcised male child, who is not circumcised in the flesh of his foreskin, that person shall be cut off from his people; he has broken My covenant" (Genesis 17:9-14).

Regardless of the pain that will result from the obedience, Abraham carried out God's instruction that same day.

So Abraham took Ishmael his son, all who were born in his house and all who were bought with his money, every male among the men of Abraham's house, and circumcised the flesh of their foreskins that very same day, as God had said to him. Abraham was ninety-nine years old when he was circumcised in the flesh of his foreskin. And Ishmael his son was thirteen years old when he was circumcised in the flesh of his foreskin. That very same day Abraham was circumcised, and his son Ishmael; and all the men of his house, born in the house or bought with money from a foreigner, were circumcised with him (Genesis 17:23-27).

Every person under authority will have series of instructions they will have to follow. Remember, you are not under spiritual authority if you do not heed instructions that you are given.

The instruction Abraham obeyed that confirmed he was truly under spiritual authority was when he was told to sacrifice his son, Isaac, to God. Guess what, Abraham obeyed that as well. He even woke up very early in the morning to obey that instruction. That would have been a good day not to hear the alarm ring! May God give you and I the grace to be truly under spiritual authority.

Now it came to pass after these things that God tested Abraham, and said to him, "Abraham!" And he said, "Here I am." Then He said, "Take now your son, your only son Isaac, whom you love, and go to the land of Moriah, and offer him there as a burnt offering on one of the mountains of which I shall tell you." So Abraham rose early in the morning and saddled his donkey, and took two of his young men with him, and Isaac his son; and he split the wood for the burnt offering, and arose and went to the place of which God had told him (Genesis 22:1-3).

For every genuine instruction we obey, there is a blessing attached.

Faith Giant 2 - Joseph

Joseph was also a man under spiritual authority. A man that is walking in holiness will also be under spiritual authority, because holiness means obeying God in all things. A man of faith will also be a man under spiritual authority, because faith without works is dead. Remember, Jesus praised the Centurion's understanding of spiritual authority by saying he had great faith.

Joseph could have easily accepted Potiphar's wife's advances, but because he was under the authority of the instructions that God gave, he refused. He also demonstrated that he was under Potiphar's authority by remaining within the confines of what his master delegated to him.

> *But he refused and said to his master's wife, "Look, my master does not know what is with me in the house, and he has committed all that he has to my hand. There is no one greater in this house than I, nor has he kept back anything from me but you, because you are his wife. How then can I do this great wickedness, and sin against God?"* (Genesis 39:8-9).

This is a man that knows he is under authority and did not disobey his master's authority as well as God's.

A person who is truly under authority will always be in authority wherever they go. Even in prison, Joseph, being a man under authority quickly became a man with authority.

> *But the Lord was with Joseph and showed him mercy, and He gave him favor in the sight of the keeper of the prison. And the keeper of the prison committed to Joseph's hand all the prisoners who were in the prison; whatever they did there, it was his doing. The keeper of the prison did not look into anything that was under Joseph's authority, because the Lord was with him; and whatever he did, the Lord made it prosper (Genesis 39:21-23).*

The Blessings of Being Under Spiritual Authority

Faith Giant 3 - Moses

Moses was a man that spoke to God face to face (Exodus 33:11). He was a man that God could trust with instructions. Yes, he failed to obey one command from God, but many of us cannot boast of a life of obedience to God like Moses. From the moment Moses answered the call to deliver the Israelites from slavery, he demonstrated what it means to be under spiritual authority.

> *Now the Lord said to Moses in Midian, "Go, return to Egypt; for all the men who sought your life are dead." Then Moses took his wife and his sons and set them on a donkey, and he returned to the land of Egypt. And Moses took the rod of God in his hand (Exodus 4:19-20).*

After he received the mandate, he continued to obey God even in the face of danger. Moses was also under the spiritual authority of his father-in-law, Jethro. There are many people who find it difficult to submit to human spiritual authority, because God has spoken to them, or because they are anointed. The fact that God has spoken to you, or personally commissioned you, does not mean do not need to be under a human spiritual authority. Moses knew that there were different levels of spiritual authority even as the ultimate authority belongs to God. Even though Moses enjoyed deep communion with God, he still listened to the sound advice of his father-in-law. Are you under any kind of spiritual authority?

And so it was, on the next day, that Moses sat to judge the people; and the people stood before Moses from morning until evening. So when Moses' father-in-law saw all that he did for the people, he said, "What is this thing that you are doing for the people? Why do you alone sit, and all the people stand before you from morning until evening?" And Moses said to his father-in-law, "Because the people come to me to inquire of God. When they have a difficulty, they come to me, and I judge between one and another; and I make known the statutes of God and His laws." So Moses' father-in-law said to him, "The thing that you do is not good. Both you and these people who are with you will surely wear yourselves out. For this thing is too much for you; you are not able to perform it by yourself. Listen now to my voice; I will give you counsel, and God will be with you: Stand before God for the people, so that you may bring the difficulties to God. And you shall teach them the statutes and the laws, and show them the way in which they must walk and the work they must do. Moreover you shall select from all the people able men, such as fear God, men of truth, hating covetousness; and place such over them to be rulers of thousands, rulers of hundreds, rulers of fifties, and rulers of tens. And let them judge the people at all times. Then it will be that every great matter they shall bring to you, but every small matter they themselves shall judge. So it will be easier for you, for they will bear the burden with you. If you do this thing, and God so commands you, then you will be able to endure, and all this people will also go to their place in peace." So Moses heeded the voice of his father-in-law and did all that he had said. And Moses chose able men out of all Israel, and made them heads over the people: rulers of thousands, rulers of hundreds, rulers of fifties, and rulers of tens. So they judged the people at all times; the hard cases they brought to Moses, but they judged every small case themselves (Exodus 18:13-26).

IV

Different Levels of Spiritual Authority

There is only one with all the authority in heaven and on the earth and that is **God the Father**. He however delegated that authority to others at different levels.

> *In the beginning God created the heavens and the earth. The earth was without form, and void; and darkness was on the face of the deep. And the Spirit of God was hovering over the face of the waters. Then God said, "Let there be light"; and there was light (Genesis 1:1-3).*

God the Father initiated the process of creation, with the Holy Spirit and Jesus Christ assisting.

The Authority of the Word (i.e. Jesus Christ)

According to the Bible, Jesus Christ is the Word of God.

In the beginning was the Word, and the Word was with God, and the Word was God. He was in the beginning with God. All things were made through Him, and without Him nothing was made that was made (John 1:1-3).

Speaking about Jesus Christ, the Bible also said…

"He is the image of the invisible God, the firstborn over all creation. For by Him all things were created that are in heaven and that are on earth, visible and invisible, whether thrones or dominions or principalities or powers. All things were created through Him and for Him (Colossians 1:15-16)

This means that Jesus Christ made all things and He is also the Word of God.

After His resurrection, Jesus said that all authority has been given to Him.

And Jesus came and spoke to them, saying, "All authority has been given to Me in heaven and on earth (Matthew 28:18).

The Word of God should be the starting point for everyone that decides to be under spiritual authority. This is the spiritual authority that must be completely obeyed at all times.

> *and that from childhood you have known the Holy Scriptures, which are able to make you wise for salvation through faith which is in Christ Jesus. All Scripture is given by inspiration of God, and is profitable for doctrine, for reproof, for correction, for instruction in righteousness, that the man of God may be complete, thoroughly equipped for every good work (2 Timothy 3:15-17).*

In order to be a Christian, you and I had to accept Jesus Christ as our personal Lord and Savior. Since Jesus Christ is the Word of God, when you became born-again, you were simply accepting the authority of the Word of God over your life. Glory to God!

All through church history, there have been cases of people submitting to the authority of "the spirit" without being under the authority of the Word. They usually end up in doctrinal error. The only way to protect yourself from false spirits is to be clearly and unapologetically under the authority of the written Word of God as explained to you by the Holy Spirit. Even Jesus Christ was under the authority of the written Word. When tempted by the devil, Jesus Christ resisted the devil's advances by stating that He was under the spiritual authority of the Word. In essence, Jesus Christ was saying that "the only reason why I will not do what you are suggesting is because the word of God has asked me not to do it" (Luke 4:4-13).

According to Psalms 138:2, God has even honored His Word more than all His name. Friends, the Word of God is the first point of call for spiritual authority. Not a spirit, not an angel, not your pastor, not your parents and not even your husband or wife. The written Word of God is the first level of God-ordained spiritual authority.

After getting married, I told my wife that from that day, our home will be governed not by whatever I feel is right to be done, but what the Word of God has clearly stated to be done. Everybody in my home is subject to the spiritual authority of the Word of God. This means that, although I am the head of the home, she has the right to challenge my decisions if it is not in line with the written Word of God.

In submitting to the authority of the Word of God, note that you must not take verses of the Bible in isolation and build doctrines based on them. A doctrine is a biblically-accepted way of life. It is a principle that God endorses as good practice and expects such of us, where necessary. For a practice to be sound doctrine, it must be backed up by two or three witnesses in the Bible. It is not enough to **find** it in the bible two or three times, it has to be in agreement with the overall theme of the Bible and in line with the clearly written nature of God.

> *This will be the third time I am coming to you. "By the mouth of two or three witnesses every word shall be established. 2 Corinthians 13:1.*

In essence, you should come across the same practice or a variation of it in at least two occurrences in the Bible. For example, it is ***not*** doctrinally sound to expect God to ask you to specifically offer your child to Him as a burnt offering, just like He asked Abraham to (Genesis 22:1-2). This is because God never asked any other Bible character to do that. God asked many Bible characters however, to make personal sacrifices to test the genuineness of their love for Him.

The Authority of the Holy Spirit

It is only after you have submitted to the authority of the Word, that you can truly be under the authority of the Holy Spirit. Jesus Christ said that the Holy Spirit will take what is His and show it to us (John 16:14). Since we know that Jesus Christ is the Word (John 1:1-3), we know that the Holy Spirit will take the Word and show it unto us.

Once you have accepted the authority of the Word of God, you are now ready to be under the spiritual authority of the Holy Spirit. The authority of the Holy Spirit must be obeyed at all times, as it aligns with the Word (if the instruction is truly from the Holy Spirit, it will always align with the Word of God). By following the leading of the Holy Spirit, we are separated from unbelievers *"For as many as are led by the Spirit of God, these are sons of God" (Romans 8:14).*

The Holy Spirit can lead us by revealing God's will for a particular situation, especially in cases where the written Word of God (i.e. logos) does not clearly address such matters. In such cases, the Holy Spirit communicates the spoken Word of God (i.e. rhema) to us in a way that we can understand.

Now in the church at Antioch there were prophets and teachers: Barnabas, Simeon called Niger, Lucius of Cyrene, Manaen (who had been brought up with Herod the tetrarch) and Saul. While they were worshiping the Lord and fasting, the Holy Spirit said, "Set apart for me Barnabas and Saul for the work to which I have called them." So after they had fasted and prayed, they placed their hands on them and sent them off (Acts 13:1-3).

To understand more about the leading of the Holy Spirit, you can read Kenneth E. Hagin's book "How You Can Be Led by the Spirit of God".

Human Authority

Even though it has been established that all authority lies with God, His Word and the Holy Spirit, it is important to note that God delegates His authority to human agents as well. God selects human agents to act on His behalf in many instances.

> *Let every soul be subject to the governing authorities. For there is no authority except from God, and the authorities that exist are appointed by God. Therefore whoever resists the authority resists the ordinance of God, and those who resist will bring judgment on themselves. Romans 13:1-2.*

All through scriptures, we see that God endorses human authority. Here are some scriptures that speak about the need to submit to human spiritual authority. Please take time to meditate on them.

Likewise you younger people, submit yourselves to your elders. Yes, all of you be submissive to one another, and be clothed with humility, for "God resists the proud, But gives grace to the humble." Therefore humble yourselves under the mighty hand of God, that He may exalt you in due time, casting all your care upon Him, for He cares for you (I Peter 5:5-7)

And Jeremiah said to the house of the Rechabites, "Thus says the Lord of hosts, the God of Israel: 'Because you have obeyed the commandment of Jonadab your father, and kept all his precepts and done according to all that he commanded you, therefore thus says the Lord of hosts, the God of Israel: "Jonadab the son of Rechab shall not lack a man to stand before Me forever" (Jeremiah 35:18-19).

Obey those who rule over you, and be submissive, for they watch out for your souls, as those who must give account. Let them do so with joy and not with grief, for that would be unprofitable for you (Hebrews 13:17).

As we have seen from earlier chapters, high flyers in the Bible were under human authority even as they were ultimately under God's authority. Human spiritual authority must be submitted to, as long as it is in line with the authority of the Word and the Holy Spirit.

There are different types of human authority.

Church Leadership (Pastors/Teachers/Evangelists, etc.)

If you belong to a local church, your human spiritual authority is the human head of that church. If you are not comfortable with the human head of the church being your spiritual authority, because of character issues, that is possibly a sign that you ought not to be in that local church. To learn more about selecting the right church, read one of the books I authored titled, "*Now That You Are Born Again, What Next?*".

God wants us to submit to the church leadership. He wants us to be obedient and submissive to those that watch and protect our souls - Hebrews 13:17.

Before starting out in ministry, I asked the Holy Spirit to tell me when I am justified as a pastor to ask a person to leave the church. I was surprised about the answer that He gave me. He said the only time it is acceptable to ask a person to leave the church is when they are rebellious. This came as a shock to me. He went on to say that this was the reason He threw the devil out of heaven. While there are disciplinary steps that could be taken when a believer refuses to repent from certain sins, the sin of rebellion can warrant a pastor asking a believer to leave a church group. There is no church leader that is perfect. There are however certain imperfections that should raise red flags for you, before you submit to their spiritual authority. Again, more information can be found in the book, *"Now That You Are Born Again, What Next?"*.

Government

God expects you and I to be under the authority of the governing bodies in every country that we find ourselves in.

> *Let every soul be subject to the governing authorities. For there is no authority except from God, and the authorities that exist are appointed by God Romans 13:1.*

> *Therefore submit yourselves to every ordinance of man for the Lord's sake, whether to the king as supreme, or to governors, as to those who are sent by him for the punishment of evildoers and for the praise of those who do good. For this is the will of God, that by doing good you may put to silence the ignorance*

*of foolish men— as free, yet not using liberty as a
cloak for vice, but as bondservants of God. Honor all
people. Love the brotherhood. Fear God. Honor the
king (I Peter 2:13-17).*

*Remind them to be subject to rulers and authorities,
to obey, to be ready for every good work (Titus 3:1).*

Biological Parents

You must understand that there was a reason why God
ensured that every human being that comes to the world
must do so, courtesy of a man's sperm and a woman's
egg. The fertilized egg continues to grow in the woman's
womb. This gives the man and woman the original right
to parent the child.

Submitting to the authority of our parents is the first
commandment with promise.

*Children, obey your parents in the Lord, for this is
right. "Honor your father and mother," which is the
first commandment with promise: "that it may be
well with you and you may live long on the earth."
And you, fathers, do not provoke your children to
wrath, but bring them up in the training and admo-
nition of the Lord (Ephesians 6:1-4).*

Mentors/Spiritual Parents

Mentors are human spiritual authorities, that help us see further. They help us to arrive at our destination sooner, and in a better shape. Isaac Newton aptly put it when he said "If I have seen further, it is by standing on the shoulders of giants". Our mentors are giants, they have seen, conquered and overcome many trials and tribulations of life. They have deeper experiences that we can learn from.

Paul was helping Timothy to understand what it means to have a spiritual father. You may have several people that instruct you in particular areas, but you will have, mainly, one spiritual father/mother or overall mentor.

I do not write these things to shame you, but as my beloved children I warn you. For though you might have ten thousand instructors in Christ, yet you do not have many fathers; for in Christ Jesus I have begotten you through the gospel (I Corinthians 4:14-15).

V

Finding Spiritual Authority

Everybody likes the power that comes from being an authority over someone else, but not everyone is qualified to possess that kind of power. One of the mistakes people make is that they qualify people's ability to be their spiritual authority, because of the position they occupy or the title they carry. The fact that a person has the title "Reverend" or "Prophet" or "Pastor" and such, does not mean they are qualified to be your spiritual authority; furthermore, it does not mean they are under God's authority or even sent by God.

> *"Beloved, do not believe every spirit, but test the spirits, whether they are of God; because many false prophets have gone out into the world"* (I John 4:1).

Through prayer, you can find out who God wants you to submit to, as your human spiritual authority.

'Call to Me, and I will answer you, and show you great and mighty things, which you do not know' (Jeremiah 33:3).

Even though prayer helps you find out what God's will is, there are other helpful ways to determine who to submit to. Since there are many false authorities out there, you will need to know how to eliminate the wrong options that readily present themselves to you.

In order to know who to submit to, we must find out what kind of person God chooses as a leader. Whoever is chosen by God to be a leader, is capable of being a spiritual authority. This is because there is no authority except that which comes from God. God delegates part of His authority to the one He chooses to be a leader.

Usually, the leaders God raises up are not the same people that the world would elevate to positions of leadership. An example is found in I Samuel 16:1-7. At this point in the Bible, Israel had a king (Saul), but he had become a great disappointment. He started well, but succumbed to folly and pride. He was no longer under God's authority, because he chose to walk in disobedience and rebellion. So Samuel was sent to anoint a new king:

The Lord said to Samuel, "How long will you mourn for Saul, since I have rejected him as king over Israel? Fill your horn with oil and be on your way; I am sending you to Jesse of Bethlehem. I have chosen one of his sons to be king." But Samuel said, "How can I go? Saul will hear about it and kill me." The Lord said, "Take a heifer with you and say, 'I have come to sacrifice to the Lord.' Invite Jesse to the sacrifice, and I will show you what to do. You are to anoint for me the one I indicate." Samuel did what the Lord said. When he arrived at Bethlehem, the elders of the town trembled when they met him. They asked, "Do you come in peace?" Samuel replied, "Yes, in peace; I have come to sacrifice to the Lord. Consecrate yourselves and come to the sacrifice with me." Then he consecrated Jesse and his sons and invited them to the sacrifice. When they arrived, Samuel saw Eliab and thought, "Surely the Lord's anointed stands here before the Lord." But the Lord said to Samuel, "Do not consider his appearance or his height, for I have rejected him. The Lord does not look at the things man looks at. Man looks at the outward appearance, but the Lord looks at the heart" (I Samuel 16:1-7).

We find later in the same story that Jesse, David's father, did not even include David in the line-up of his sons (verse 8-11) when Prophet Samuel requested to see his sons; he was an afterthought to Jesse. Qualification for leadership is not measured by inches or pounds or degrees or background or even accolades. What does God look for? Why is it that when Jesse and Samuel were looking at Eliab, God was looking at David? God's qualifications for leadership are evident in verse 7 *"...man looks at the outward appearance, but the Lord looks at the heart" (1 Samuel 16:7).*

Even the prophet Samuel was fooled. When he looked at Jesse's oldest son Eliab, he naturally assumed that God must have chosen this noble and sturdy young man to be the Lord's anointed leader. But the Lord makes it clear in this passage that the people he chooses to do great things for him are called on the basis of inward character, not on the basis of outward impressiveness alone. The devil can conjure up outward impressiveness to deceive people, but he cannot develop lasting inward character in a person. God is not only interested in what we do, but He is interested in who we are. In fact, the things that impress human beings are usually not impressive to God. The thing that God looks for is the quality of a good heart.

Why is the condition of a person's heart such a big deal? Don't we often hear about the difference between a leader's private life and their ability to perform well on the job? All we have to do is look one generation from David to see the tragedy that awaits a leader, whose heart is not right before God. In I Kings 3:6, Solomon is engaged in a conversation with the Lord. Solomon says, *"You have shown great kindness to your servant, my father David, because he was faithful to you and righteous and upright in heart. You have continued this great kindness to him and have given him a son to sit on his throne this very day"*. Clearly, Solomon began his reign well, but he was half-hearted.

Just a few chapters later we read *"For it came to pass, when Solomon was old, that his wives turned away his heart after other gods: and his heart was not perfect with the Lord his God, as was the heart of David his father. For Solomon went after Ashtoreth the goddess of the Zidonians, and after Milcom the abomination of the Ammonites. And Solomon did evil in the sight of the Lord, and went not fully after the Lord, as did David his father" (I Kings 11:4-6).*

Before submitting your will to another (being under spiritual authority), you must do a thorough "background" check of the person, not after you have. Since there is no organization that can do this for you, you will have to go through this on your own with the help of the Holy Spirit.

There is no exhaustive list out there, but there are a few questions you should ask yourself concerning the person you want to submit to:

1. The Authority Question

- "Am I submitting to God in a man or am I simply submitting to a man?"
  - ○ Even though God expects you to submit to human authority, He still expects you to be absolutely under His authority. Nobody must take the place of God in your life. Ensure that you are not being swayed by a person's charismatic nature, hence the submission to them. The Bible tells us that anyone who place their trust in another man is cursed (Jeremiah 17:5). Even though you are in submission to human authority, your trust must always and absolutely remain in God.

- Is this person under God's authority?
  - Before submitting your will to another, ensure that person has submitted their will to God. The person can only lead you to God, if he walks with Him. The Holy Spirit said this to me a few years ago "Anyone who tries to lead without being led will mislead and be misled". If you submit your will to a person who is not under God's authority, you stand the risk of been led astray.
- Is this person under any other human authority?
  - All who claim to submit to God's direct authority, but reject delegated authority are nonetheless under the force of rebellion. Since God compares rebellion to the sin of witchcraft (I Samuel 15:23), you stand the risk of been under the authority of a rebellious person. Find out who they are submitting to, and check that person out if you can. For out of the abundance that they receive from that person, they will also give unto you!

2. The Character Question

- Does this person model acceptable character?

- ○ Your spiritual authority is a mirror of how you will look like after a sustained period of mentorship.
- Do you like the character traits you see in that person right now?
  - ○ Do you admire their character traits?
  - ○ Does God approve of what He sees in that person right now? The Bible tells us the fruit of the Holy Spirit are: love, joy, peace, long-suffering, kindness, goodness, faithfulness, gentleness and self-control (Galatians 5:22-23). If you do not see the fruits of the Holy Spirit operating in their life, **BEWARE!** That may be a wolf in sheep's clothing, disguising himself or herself.
- When you look at the person's life in general, does it encourage you to press on, to keep going, to keep "your hands on the plough"?
  - ○ A spiritual authority has to tow a fine line between "showing you love" and "pushing you away from your comfort zone".
- Do they have the moral strength to correct you when you go astray? Or are they afraid of offending you?

○ Jesus Christ modeled this in the way He led His disciples. In many cases, He scolded them when they acted improperly. This scolding only drew them closer to Him, because He already demonstrated His love for them on several occasions.

3. The Competency Question

- Does this person have what it takes to lead me?
  - ○ Character alone does not qualify a person to be your spiritual authority. They need to be duly empowered. Jesus had the empowerment of the Holy Spirit to lead His disciples.
- What kind of gifts of the Holy Spirit do you see the person demonstrating? I Corinthians 12:1-31.
  - ○ To be a spiritual authority over another, a person needs to constantly operate in the gifts of the Holy Spirit; since it is not by natural power or by might that we get spiritual things done. A person that wants to be a spiritual authority over another must be capable of drawing upon the gifts of the Holy Spirit to lead another.
- Are they knowledgeable enough to lead?

- o Solomon realized the supremacy of wisdom as a trait for a successful leader and he asked God for it when the opportunity arose (I Kings 3:1-15).

- Do they demonstrate sound judgement in their affairs?

  - o It is not enough to be "wise". The person should demonstrate the operation of that wisdom, by the trail of good decisions that they make. Solomon proved the wisdom deposit in him by his sound judgement (I Kings 3:16-28). Our lives are made up of decisions. We make decisions on who to marry, what to wear, how to act in challenging times and other important decisions. Watch and see the soundness of their decision making. Nobody is infallible. Even a spiritual authority is capable of making mistakes. Do not judge a person, because they made a few bad decisions. All I am saying here is that there has to be trail of good decisions that the person has made and keeps making, to ensure they are capable of leading you right. The Bible states that if a person does not know how to rule his own house, how will he take care of the church of God? (I Timothy 3:5). The Bible also says that those who want to become a deacon in the church must first be tested (I Timothy 5:10). Since you are part of the body of Christ, hence the church, these scriptures apply to you. The affairs of your life should not be their test bed for learning how to make sound decisions. They must have a proven track record of making sound decisions.

- Are there gifts from the Holy Spirit the person possess that you strongly admire (or covet)? (I Corinthians 12:31)
  - o Peter knew Jesus walked in the supernatural, because Jesus demonstrated it to them many times. On one occasion, Peter even asked Jesus if He could allow him walk on water as well. For a spiritual authority relationship to thrive, you must strongly desire the gifts that the person operates in. You must see the person as being way ahead of you in many areas. This will enable you to genuinely submit to their authority.

4. The Willingness Question

- Is it mutual?

- ○ Being under a person's spiritual authority is a relationship. Like every successful relationship, there has to be mutual consent. If you are the only person desiring the relationship, it will not work. Can two walk together except they agree? (Amos 3:3)
- Is there a sacrifice?
  - ○ Are they willing to go above and beyond in order to lead you? Being a spiritual authority is like being a shepherd. There are lots of sacrifices involved in being a shepherd. Has the person demonstrated they are ready to go above and beyond for you? In John 3:16, we see that God went above and beyond to prove his love for us. He gave His only begotten Son for us. For any sacrifice to be worth it, it has to be based on love. Does the person love you? Since love never fails (I Corinthians 13:8), the bond of love will keep the spiritual authority relationship through thick and thin. Jesus wept over the death of Lazarus and the people said "See how He loved him" (John 11:36). It is not enough for you to love your spiritual authority. They must love you back.

- Are they open?
  - Your spiritual authority has to be one that is open to you. They should be one that do not hide their past mistakes. They are willing to share intimate aspects of their life when needed, appropriate and necessary.

VI

Blessings for Being Under Spiritual Authority

God never asks His children to do something without attaching a blessing to it. The command to submit to spiritual authority is a powerful one. This means that we can be controlled, directed or instructed against our will and God will expect obedience from us. God's commandments are not grievous, when we follow them the way God designed it, not according to our own ideas.

According to scriptures, we were redeemed to enjoy the blessings of Abraham.

He redeemed us in order that the blessing given to Abraham might come to the Gentiles through Christ Jesus, so that by faith we might receive the promise of the Spirit (Galatians 3:14).

God spoke these blessings to Abraham.

"I will make you into a great nation, and I will bless you; I will make your name great, and you will be a blessing. I will bless those who bless you, and whoever curses you I will curse; and all peoples on earth will be blessed through you" (Genesis 12:2-3).

For these blessings to materialize, he had to be under spiritual authority. Remember, we defined spiritual authority as being under God's authority directly or indirectly. We see in these instances below, how Abraham demonstrated his obedience to God by taking action.

So Abram departed as the Lord had spoken to him, and Lot went with him. And Abram was seventy-five years old when he departed from Haran (Genesis 12:4).

Now it came to pass after these things that God tested Abraham, and said to him, "Abraham!" And he said, "Here I am." Then He said, "Take now your son, your only son Isaac, whom you love, and go to the land of Moriah, and offer him there as a burnt offering on one of the mountains of which I shall tell you." So Abraham rose early in the morning and saddled his donkey, and took two of his young men with him, and Isaac his son; and he split the wood for the burnt offering, and arose and went to the place of which God had told him (Genesis 22:1-3).

Moses is another example in scriptures that enjoyed the blessing of walking in the fullness of his calling because he was under God's authority. He demonstrated he was under spiritual authority by:

- Obeying God's written instructions (Laws).
- Obeying the leading of the Spirit of God.
- Being under the authority of his father-in-law.

Another example is Ruth. For Ruth to get married to Boaz, she had to follow the specific instructions given to her by Naomi — her mother-in-law. Naomi gave her specific instructions on how to conduct herself and the result was beneficial to Ruth (Book of Ruth chapters 1-4). Remember, there is no authority without control. That is why it takes a humble person to be under spiritual authority. Whenever you are truly under spiritual authority, it is always you benefiting, not your spiritual authority. For Esther to become the next queen and play a huge role in rescuing the Israelites, she had to follow the instructions that Mordecai gave her.

Every high-flyer is a person under clear, God-ordained spiritual authority. You can never reach the top in your area of calling without practically being under your God-ordained spiritual authority.

Psalms 23 is a summary of the blessings we enjoy for being under spiritual authority. Let's explore Psalm 23 together. It starts with a clear declaration of being under God's spiritual authority.

Verse 1 - *The Lord is my shepherd; I shall not want.*

- It means you are under God's direct and indirect spiritual authority. A shepherd actively leads the sheep. This verse is David's bold declaration that he is under God's authority.
- Before you begin to confess that you shall not want, ask yourself the question "Is the Lord my shepherd?". Does the Lord lead me and I follow? If so, you are qualified to live in the realm where there is no lack and no toil. It is a realm where all your needs are met by God, who is your shepherd.

Have you ever heard of a new recruit to the army that goes about soliciting funds to buy military uniform or guns or bullets? The military makes provision for all the needs of their recruits. It is the same for the one that is led by the Great Shepherd. All their needs are supernaturally met by God.

Verse 2 - He makes me to lie down in green pastures; He leads me beside the still waters.

- The definition of spiritual authority is that your will is submitted to another. The shepherd is able to make you do something. It means that you are not stubborn. You are a sheep that is teachable, not a goat that is unteachable. Can your shepherd make you do something or you only do what you want to do? Can you be led, or you only go where you want to go? This verse shows that being under a real God-ordained spiritual authority entitles you to lie down in green pastures and enjoy still waters. It means you enjoy abundance everywhere you are and peace in every situation.

Verse 3 - He restores my soul; He leads me in the paths of righteousness For His name's sake.

- God restores the soul of those that are under His direct and indirect authority. God (or a human spiritual authority) is bound to restore the souls of those under His authority. Being under spiritual authority always positions you for good things. You will be led in the paths of righteousness, not unrighteousness. The name of the authority you are under is on the line. That is why the verse says "for His name's sake".

Verse 4 - Yea, though I walk through the valley of the shadow of death, I will fear no evil; For You are with me; Your rod and Your staff, they comfort me.

- God is with those under His spiritual authority. No matter what they go through, they go through it with God on their side. Those under spiritual authority enjoy divine presence. They ought to know no fear because of God's abiding presence. You see all through these verses that the shepherd is equally committed to the relationship as the sheep is.

Verse 5 - You prepare a table before me in the presence of my enemies; You anoint my head with oil; My cup runs over.

- God makes abundant provision available to those under His authority. He always replenishes their anointing in a manner that causes an overflow. Those under spiritual authority enjoy overflow. They are assured of divine revelations, both directly from God to them and from God through their human spiritual authority(ies). There is never dryness. Even in the midst of attacks, opposition and battles, they are feasting.

Verse 6 - Surely goodness and mercy shall follow me all the days of my life; And I will dwell in the house of the Lord forever.

- Those under spiritual authority have goodness and mercy following them everywhere they go; this is guaranteed to happen all the days of their lives. They have a good report all the days of their lives. There is no up and down. There are only continuous transformations. It is always a move from glory to glory. Those under authority have exercised their will to dwell in the house of the Lord forever (i.e. remaining under God's authority forever and ever). If this is you, shout hallelujah!

Some definite blessings you will enjoy from being under spiritual authority are:

You will have authority

- *And being found in appearance as a man, He humbled Himself and became obedient to the point of death, even the death of the cross. Therefore God also has highly exalted Him and given Him the name which is above every name, that at the name of Jesus every knee should bow, of those in heaven, and of those on earth, and of those under the earth, and that every tongue should confess that Jesus Christ is Lord, to the glory of God the Father (Philippians 2:8-11).*

- *He who is faithful in what is least is faithful also in much; and he who is unjust in what is least is unjust also in much. Therefore if you have not been faithful in the unrighteous mammon, who will commit to your trust the true riches? And if you have not been faithful in what is another man's, who will give you what is your own? Luke 16:10-12.*

You will be empowered to resist the devil

- *Therefore submit to God. Resist the devil and he will flee from you (James 4:7).*

You will always know what to do

- If God does not reveal to you directly, He will reveal the steps you need to take to your spiritual authority. Example is Jethro advising Moses on how to delegate tasks. You would have expected God to share this with Moses directly (Exodus 18:13-26) but instead, the wisdom came through Moses' father-in-law.

You will be protected

- Being under authority assures our protection from the storms of life. Lot and his family were rescued because he was under Abraham's authority - Genesis 14: 1-24.
- Jesus's disciples were protected on many occasions because they were under Jesus' spiritual authority. An example is in Mark 4:35-41.
- The General Overseer of The Redeemed Christian Church of God, Pastor E.A. Adeboye, shared his

personal experience that clearly illustrates this point. Immediately he became born again, the Holy Spirit instructed him to ensure he was under the authority of his Pastor, Pa. Akindayomi — the then General Overseer and Founder of the Redeemed Christian Church of God — this he endeavored to do immediately. Sometime in 1977, his country was hosting a festival of Arts and Culture, which he considered to be a guise for idol worship. Grieved by that event, he got an idea he believed originated from God, to organize a different event coinciding with that festival to glorify God. He immediately shared the idea with Pa. Akindayomi, who completely agreed with the idea and instructed him to proceed. After getting the go ahead, he sent out invitation letters to ministers and other Pastors in the Redeemed Christian Church of God denomination. Not quite long after, he received a scathing letter from one of the Pastors in his denomination, cursing and accusing him of scheming this event just to become popular, among other false accusations. On getting this letter, he went to Pa. Akindayomi to report the false accusations. Expecting that Pa. Akindayomi will immediately call the Pastor to order, and even discipline him; he was disappointed when he was told by Pa. Akindayomi to apologize to the Pastor, who made the false accusations against him. After struggling with that instruction for some time, he was reminded by the Holy Spirit that he was meant to submit to the authority of the General Overseer, which meant heeding his instructions and counsel. He went on to apologize to the Pastor and went ahead with the planning and execution of the event. Sometime later, events unfolded that made the said Pastor to confess that he was certain he would be going to hell and had determined to take three people with him. The three people he intended to take with him included Pa. Akindayomi and Pastor E.A. Adeboye. When this statement was made, Pa. Akindayomi reminded Pastor E.A. Adeboye why he told him to apologize when he was offended by that Pastor. God used Pastor E.A. Adeboye's spiritual authority to save him from the trap of offence and to the glory of God, he is still going strong till today.

You will have a long life and things will be well with you

- *Children, obey your parents in the Lord, for this is right. "Honor your father and mother," which is the first commandment with promise: "that it may be well with you and you may live long on the earth (Ephesians 6:1–3).*

You will bring delight to the Lord

- *"Children, obey your parents in all things: for this is well pleasing unto the Lord" (Colossians 3:20).*

You will operate at a higher level

- Apollos already had a good report that he was mighty in the scriptures. One would have thought that he would not have any need to be under spiritual authority. Remember, no matter how good you currently are, being under your God-ordained spiritual authority will make you better.

"Now a certain Jew named Apollos, born at Alexandria, an eloquent man and mighty in the Scriptures, came to Ephesus. This man had been instructed in the way of the Lord; and being fervent in spirit, he spoke and taught accurately the things of the Lord, though he knew only the baptism of John.

So he began to speak boldly in the synagogue. When Aquila and Priscilla heard him, they took him aside and explained to him the way of God more accurately. And when he desired to cross to Achaia, the brethren wrote, exhorting the disciples to receive him; and when he arrived, he greatly helped those who had believed through grace; for he vigorously refuted the Jews publicly, showing from the Scriptures that Jesus is the Christ" (Acts 18:24-28).

VII

Remaining Under Spiritual Authority

Making a decision to be under spiritual authority is relatively easier than remaining under that authority for the rest of your life.

The Case of King Saul

The story of King Saul teaches us that one may start well but end up badly if not careful. Scripture clearly states, *"12 Therefore let him who thinks he stands take heed lest he fall" (I Corinthians 10:12).* King Saul was the first king in Israel. He had the opportunity to be a pacesetter. He was anointed by one of the greatest and most powerful prophets in Israel's history. He was physically attractive. His nation overwhelmingly wanted him to rule over them. Regardless of all these he had going for him, Saul more or less eventually failed — by not remaining under God's direct authority and His delegated spiritual authority, Prophet Samuel.

I Samuel 9 introduces us to Saul. He was a man under authority. He honored his biological father, Kish, by going above and beyond to obey his instruction. He also honored Prophet Samuel by not going to see him empty-handed. Saul's downward spiral from his kingship began with his unauthorized sacrificial offering.

> So Saul said, "Bring a burnt offering and peace offerings here to me." And he offered the burnt offering. Now it happened, as soon as he had finished presenting the burnt offering, that Samuel came; and Saul went out to meet him, that he might greet him. And Samuel said, "What have you done?" Saul said, "When I saw that the people were scattered from me, and that you did not come within the days appointed, and that the Philistines gathered together at Michmash, then I said, 'The Philistines will now come down on me at Gilgal, and I have not made supplication to the Lord.' Therefore I felt compelled, and offered a burnt offering" (1 Samuel 13:9-12).

We need to always remember that God does not condone rebellion. In this case, Saul overstepped his authority as king, to offer the sacrifice to God. A combination of fear and pride "compelled" Saul to break God's clear instruction on who should offer that sacrifice to Him. Saul's spiral downward continued as he failed to eliminate all of the Amalekites and their livestocks as commanded by God in I Samuel 15:1-35. He disregarded a direct order from God and decided to spare the life of King Agag along with some of the choice livestocks. This disobedience caused God to withdraw His Spirit from Saul, in what will be arguably one of the saddest occurrences in Scripture.

Nuggets from the Fall of Saul

- Remain humble under God's direct and indirect authority.
- Even when you do not understand, obey. The understanding can come afterwards.
- Understand the extent of your authority and remain within the limits of your authority.
- All through a life of being under spiritual authority, you will make mistakes. Learn to say "I'm sorry".

- No matter how high you rise, or how successful you become, make sure you always submit to the authority God has placed over your life.
- No matter how high you rise, or how successful you become, remember that there is someone always higher than you, that God expects you to submit to.
- Since all authority is from God, He reserves the right to withdraw His authority from anyone that is no longer subject to Him, directly or indirectly, through human spiritual authority.

The Case of King David

King David came to power as a result of the failures of King Saul. He was a man after God's own heart, but with his fair share of mistakes. He was however, a man clearly and consistently under authority. His story should remind us of the scripture *"And let us not grow weary while doing good, for in due season we shall reap if we do not lose heart"* *(Galatians 6:9).*

David also started out being submissive to his biological father. He was dedicated to the assignment he was given. He even risked his life on a number of occasions in order to save the sheep he was watching over in I Samuel 17:34-36.

The visit of the greatest prophet in Israel's history did not compel him to disobey his father's instruction to watch over the sheep. Even after a major breakthrough of being selected to be king Saul's armour bearer, he was still under the authority of his biological father in I Samuel 17:14-18. When Goliath mounted pressure on King Saul and his army, David was not compelled to disrespect the King. When David had another monumental breakthrough by defeating Goliath, he still remained under King Saul's authority. Even after Saul tried to kill him several times, David still recognized and submitted to Saul's authority (although, he exercised wisdom, by leaving Saul's presence and physically protecting himself). Fast-forward to when David ascended the throne, he was under Nathan, the Prophet's authority.

On one occasion, David disobeyed God. He sinned against God. He came out of spiritual authority by succumbing to his fleshy desire to sleep with Bathsheba and kill her husband Uriah. Even though this was a grave sin, David's comeback is worth learning from. He immediately repented and asked God for forgiveness in II Samuel 12:13.

On another occasion, David flouted God's instruction not to number the troops of Israel and Judah. Again, because of his humility and submission to God's authority, he immediately repented in II Samuel 24:10. The life of King David shows us that no matter how great you become, you can only sustain that greatness by remaining under God's direct and indirect (delegated human) authority. Remember, you are truly under God's direct and delegated spiritual authority when you choose to follow the instructions as they are given.

If there is no one you are obeying in the name of Christ, your salvation and walk with God is questionable!

Nuggets from the Success of David

- David was a genuine lover of God. He demonstrated his love for God, by his giving and service to God. By that love, he easily submitted to spiritual authority.
- Humility is the key to remaining under spiritual authority.
- No matter how great you become, never lose sight of where you were before God elevated you.
- Always sincerely resist every attempt of people to lift you up more than is due.
- Genuinely honor and respect those God has put as authority over your life.

- Genuinely recognize the gifts of those God has put over you.
- Accept the implication of the mistakes that you make, and receive the scolding with love.

Some Things to Watch Out for As You Remain Under Authority

Handling Correction

- Beginning the journey of being under spiritual authority usually starts out "sweet" until corrections or scoldings starts coming. Your spiritual authority can sometimes scold you based on their personality type or the hurt they feel as a result of your mistake. Resist the urge to hold on to words that were spoken that might have been hurtful to you. Your spiritual authority, though ahead of you in many ways, is still human and can respond to emotions just like you would. Do you know that on many occasions, God "disowned" the children of Israel because of something they did? If they allowed those words to keep them from seeking God again, they would have missed out.

- One of the proofs that you are truly under spiritual authority is the corrections that come as a result of the mistakes we make. The Bible states that God only corrects those He loves. The same goes for a true spiritual authority. They are not afraid of offending you by telling you the truth, in love.

- The truth is that no correction feels good when it is being received. Your flesh will always want to find a reason to dispute and justify the correctness of your actions, or why the correction was improperly done. Resist the urge to be defensive. The place of authority is a place of safety. Corrections makes you feel exposed, but remember that you are in a safe place.

- Meditate on this passage and let it minister to you.

For whom the Lord loves He chastens, And scourges every son whom He receives." 7 If you endure chastening, God deals with you as with sons; for what son is there whom a father does not chasten? 8 But if you are without chastening, of which all have become partakers, then you are illegitimate and not sons.9 Furthermore, we have had human fathers who corrected us, and we paid them respect. Shall we not much more readily be in subjection to the Father of spirits and live? 10 For they indeed for a few days chastened us as seemed best to them, but He for our profit, that we may be partakers of His holiness. 11

Now no chastening seems to be joyful for the present, but painful; nevertheless, afterward it yields the peaceable fruit of righteousness to those who have been trained by it (Hebrews 12:6-11).

Avoiding Offence

- As with most relationships, there will be trying times. There will be times when it seems like you have been forsaken or you are not being given the attention that you need or your spiritual authority is not coming through for you. Remember, this applies to God as well. There are times it will seem like you are walking alone. There are times when you might be falsely accused. There may even be disagreements over doctrine, approach and decisions. In essence, watch out for anything that will cause you to be offended at your spiritual authority. This is a trap of the devil. He tricked Job into believing that God inflicted the troubles he faced on him. He even moved Job's wife to tempt him to curse God and die.

Honor

- Learn to continually honor the authority that God has placed over your life. The more you genuinely honor them, the easier it will be to submit to their authority. "*Let the elders who rule well be counted worthy of double honor, especially those who labor in the word and doctrine". (1 Timothy 5:7)*

o   You can honor them through your speech. Ensure that no corrupt criticism is allowed in your heart or spoken against them, directly or indirectly. Excitedly and confidently reaffirm to all who will listen that you are under their spiritual authority. Remember, you are submitting to them because of God in them.

o   You can honor them by your giving. Regularly give them gifts to show your appreciation for their sacrifice and positive contribution in your life. The laborer is worthy of his wages (*I Timothy 5:18)*. A true God-ordained spiritual authority does not need what you have. .

o   You can also honor them by your service. There are times when they will need your assistance. Willingly offer it. David demonstrated he was under his father's authority by running errands for him. Strive to help them achieve their God-given vision. Think of ways to serve them in areas they need to be served. The Bible says that Elisha poured water on the hands of Elijah. This simply means Elisha served Elijah, his spiritual authority (*2 Kings 3:11*).

Renewing the Vows

- Just like it is advisable to renew wedding vows, it is helpful to renew your vows to be under spiritual authority. As often as you can, re-establish your commitment to be under the spiritual authority. The advantage of renewing vows is that it rekindles the passion that made you submit to the spiritual authority in the first place and reminds you of why you chose to be under authority in the first place.

When it is okay to change your spiritual authority

- There are specific circumstances that would warrant you changing or removing yourself from under a human spiritual authority.
  - The ultimate authority in heaven and on the earth is God. If a spiritual authority is no longer under God's authority, they have lost their right to be your spiritual authority.
  - Disagreements over doctrine does not count as a reason not to submit to a spiritual authority.

Apostle Paul had a disagreement with Apostle Peter over doctrine and Peter's attitude towards the gentile Christians, when the Jewish Christians were present. This did not cause Paul to reject Peter's spiritual authority.

When there is a clash of authorities

• There are times when there will be a clash of instructions. This means that a human spiritual authority can ask you to do something different from what God has said to you. In a case like this, you will want to be fully assured that God has spoken to you. If you are fully assured, you should respectfully decline the instruction from the human spiritual authority. God reserves the right to completely direct our lives. Do not be afraid of offending your spiritual authority in this case. If they are truly walking with God, they will recognize that you made the right decision. This should not cause you to despise them or their authority. There are times when God hides His plans even from those who walk with Him, in order to show that He alone is God. Remember, God's authority is supreme and when there is a clash between what God has said through His Word or Spirit and what a human authority is saying, the Word and Spirit of God take preeminence and should be obeyed in all totality.

o On one occasion, Jesus did not go with His parents because He wanted to obey God i.e. go about God's business (Luke 2:41-50).

o Another example is the story of a prophet in I Kings 13:1-34. The prophet disobeyed the King, because what he asked him to do contradicted God's instructions. He however, fell to the cunningness of the old prophet who deceived him to disobey God. In this example, God expected the prophet to disobey the instruction of the old prophet.

o The Apostles also demonstrated this doctrine. They were instructed by the Sanhedrin not to preach in the name of Jesus anymore. Here was their response *"But Peter and John answered and said to them, "Whether it is right in the sight of God to listen to you more than to God, you judge. For we cannot but speak the things which we have seen and heard" (Acts 4:19-20).*

Hindrances to being under Spiritual Authority

The devil has come to steal, kill and destroy. Whatever he attempts to steal must be of great value. Whatever you find your flesh desiring or running away from, must be of great value to you. The devil does not attempt to steal something that is worthless or priceless.

The moment you find yourself resisting something that is clearly ordained by God, you are walking on a dangerous ground. You are playing with fire and it will burn.

There are two main hindrances that can stop you from being under spiritual authority. They are lack of knowledge and pride.

Lack of knowledge

Many people avoid being under authority because they do not know what is in it for them. If you understand that this is solely for your advantage, you will completely embrace it.

It is written, *"My people are destroyed for lack of knowledge. Because you have rejected knowledge, I also will reject you from being priest for Me; Because you have forgotten the law of your God, I also will forget your children" (Hosea 4:6).*

The devil thrives on the ignorance of believers. That is why he is able to convince them that what is good is actually dangerous. Why do you eagerly submit to the authority of your supervisor at work, even though you know they clearly do not like you; but cautiously submit to spiritual authority, even after they have consistently demonstrated their love for you?

Lack of knowledge does not only mean "not knowing anything", but it also means not knowing enough of something, for it to be useful. Many of the people I encounter that argue about spiritual things are those that just know enough to be dangerous to themselves and others.

The revelation of the truth is the solution to ignorance. As you read on, I pray that every misconception of spiritual authority will be dispelled in Jesus' name.

Pride

The human race is naturally very prideful. Individuals naturally want to boss everyone else around. The implication of this is that in their natural state, nobody will like to be under another's authority. This has brought about a proliferation of organizations or movements with rebellious intentions.

According to the Merriam-Webster dictionary, pride is "a feeling that you are more important or better than other people".

The Bible says the following about pride:

"These six things the Lord hates, Yes, seven are an abomination to Him: A proud look," (Proverbs 6:16-17).

Everyone proud in heart is an abomination to the Lord; Though they join forces, none will go unpunished (Proverbs 16:5).

Pride goes before destruction, And a haughty spirit before a fall. Better to be of a humble spirit with the lowly, Than to divide the spoil with the proud (Proverbs 16:18-19).

It is pride that makes a person not to ask for help, when they desperately need one. It is pride that makes a person resist help, just because they do not want to attribute their success to another. Get off that high horse immediately, and put yourself under spiritual authority for your maximum benefit. I command every spirit of pride to get out of you in Jesus' name. Receive grace to humble yourself in Jesus' name.

Epilogue

Yes, it is true that many have abused their position of spiritual authority. Notwithstanding, God still has many blessings in store for those that choose to remain under His direct or indirect spiritual authority.

A true spiritual authority has nothing to gain from being your authority, it is you and I that have all to gain. Strive and ensure that you stay under spiritual authority, no matter the amount of success you have.

Many have gone out and acquired success, but soon lost it all because of the mistake of not being under spiritual authority. I believe that God connected you with this book to enable you enjoy consistent success in all that you do. Apply what you have learnt from this book. Refer to it time and time again. Allow the Holy Spirit to teach you more about spiritual authority.

May the God and Father of our Lord Jesus Christ continually be with you both now and forever more. May you succeed where others have failed. May God lead you to your spiritual authority and grant you the grace to remain under His direct and indirect spiritual authority, Amen.

A Sinner's Prayer to Receive
Jesus Christ as Savior

Dear Heavenly Father,

I come to You in the Name of Jesus Christ.

You said in Your Word, "Whosoever shall call upon the name of the Lord shall be saved" (Romans 10:13). I am calling on Your Name, so I know You have saved me now.

You also said that "if you confess with your mouth the Lord Jesus and believe in your heart that God has raised Him from the dead, you will be saved. For with the heart one believes unto righteousness, and with the mouth confession is made unto salvation" (Romans 10:9-10). I believe in my heart Jesus Christ is the Son of God. I believe that He was raised from the dead for my justification, and I confess Him now as my Lord and Savior.

Thank you Lord, because now, I am saved!

Thank You Lord, because I know you have heard my prayer. Thank You Lord, because I am now born again.

Signed _____

Date _____

About the Author

Emmanuel Adewusi is the Founding and Lead Pastor of Cornerstone Christian Church Of God.

Called into ministry with the mandate to "bring restoration and transformation to all by teaching and preaching the gospel of Jesus Christ", he is passionate to see lives restored and transformed to the way God intended from the beginning of creation. He has a passion for the full counsel of the word of God, fellowship with the Holy Spirit and being under spiritual authority.

He hosts several *COME AND SEE* Conferences, with the goal to reach lost souls for Jesus Christ.

He is also the author of "*Now That You Are Born Again, What Next?*".

Emmanuel Adewusi is joyfully married to his wife, Ibukun Adewusi, and together, they are building a thriving family.

Contact the Author

I would be delighted to hear from you!

For further inquiries, please contact the author via email: emmanuel.adewusi@cccghq.org.

For online sermons, please visit www.cccghq.org.

NOTES

NOTES

NOTES

Made in United States
North Haven, CT
23 March 2024